21st
Century
Skills Library

ANIMAL INVADERS

SEA LAMPREY

Barbara A. Somervill

Cherry Lake Publishing
Ann Arbor, Michigan

Published in the United States of America by Cherry Lake Publishing
Ann Arbor, Michigan
www.cherrylakepublishing.com

Content Adviser: Marc Gaden, PhD, Communications Officer and Legislative Liaison,
Great Lakes Fishery Commission, Ann Arbor, Michigan

Please note: Our map is as up-to-date as possible at the time of publication.

Photo Credits: Cover and pages 1 and 18, Courtesy of U.S. Fish and Wildlife Service
Archive, U.S. Fish and Wildlife Service, Bugwood.org; page 4, ©iStockphoto.
com/annedehaas; pages 7, 8, 11, and 23, Courtesy of T. Lawrence, GLFC; page 14,
©blickwinkelAlamy; page 17, ©Kari Niemeläinen/Alamy; page 21, ©iStockphoto.com/
Jarrod1; page 25, ©AP Photo/John L. Russell; page 27, ©AP Photo/The Knoxville News
Sentinel, Amy Smotherman

Map by XNR Productions Inc.

Library of Congress Cataloging-in-Publication Data
Somervill, Barbara A.
Sea lamprey / by Barbara A. Somervill.
    p. cm.—(Animal invaders)
Includes index.
ISBN-13: 978-1-60279-240-1
ISBN-10: 1-60279-240-2
1. Sea lamprey—Juvenile literature. I. Title. II. Series.
QL638.25.P48S66 2009
597'.2—dc22   2008000802

*Cherry Lake Publishing would like to acknowledge the work of
The Partnership for 21st Century Skills.
Please visit www.21stcenturyskills.org for more information.*

TABLE OF CONTENTS

CHAPTER ONE
Evil Suckers!   4

CHAPTER TWO
Life of a Lamprey   7

CHAPTER THREE
Fishy Invader   13

CHAPTER FOUR
Many Problems   18

CHAPTER FIVE
Controlling the Sea Lampreys   23

Map   28

Glossary   30

For More Information   31

Index   32

About the Author   32

EVIL SUCKERS!

A sea lamprey has attached to this salmon swimming upstream in the Great Lakes.

In the early 1920s, a fisherman in Lake Erie caught more than he bargained for. His first catch was a walleye. But it had an open wound on its side. It looked like something had taken a neatly shaped bite out of the walleye.

The fisherman threw the walleye back and cast his line again. He caught four fish and then hauled in a nice-sized lake trout—with a gaping, oval wound on its side. The fisherman was puzzled. What could be doing this to Lake Erie's fish?

The fisherman's next catch supplied the answer. He hauled in a large whitefish called a cisco—with a creature that looked like an eel attached to it. Its oddly shaped, oval mouth was firmly set in the cisco's side.

The creature was an invasive **species** called the sea lamprey. An invasive species is an animal or plant not native to an area whose introduction harms the local environment, economy, or human health. This animal invader would breed in great numbers and affect all the Great Lakes.

One of North America's most valuable resources is the Great Lakes. Originally carved out by huge bodies of ice

moving slowly over millions of years, the five Great Lakes are some of the largest in the world. They mark part of the border between the United States and Canada. They also provide food, drinking water, and fun for more than 40 million people.

Today, **fisheries** in the Great Lakes produce $4 billion each year. Thousands of workers depend on fishing, tourism, and lake management to earn their living.

Keeping a healthy environment in all five Great Lakes is hard work. The fight against pollution, loss of **habitat**, and invasive species is never-ending.

CHAPTER TWO

LIFE OF A LAMPREY

*The mouth of a sea lamprey is full of little teeth
that it uses to attach to other creatures.*

Sea lampreys are truly ugly suckers! They live by attaching themselves to **prey** and sucking out their body fluids. These jawless fish are called **parasites**. Lampreys first lived hundreds of millions of years ago, long before dinosaurs roamed the land.

Seven gill pouches on each side of the body help the sea lamprey breathe.

The adult lamprey measures from 12 to 30 inches (30 to 76 centimeters) long. It usually weighs a little more than 0.5 pound (227 grams). An adult lamprey has a gray-blue to brownish back, a lighter underside, and silvery sides.

The sea lamprey does not have a typical fish body. It has no ribs, no paired fins, and no true gills. Lampreys breathe through seven pairs of gill pouches.

A sea lamprey's most unusual feature is its mouth. The mouth has no jaws but plenty of teeth. A lamprey has 10 to 12 circular rows of teeth. The rows of teeth allow the lamprey to latch on and hold fast to prey. Teeth also cover the lamprey's tongue. These teeth rub away scales and expose the prey's flesh so the lamprey can get to the body fluids it needs.

A sea lamprey passes through three stages during its life. It starts as a **larva**, then turns into a **transformer**, and finally becomes an adult.

Producing young starts as late spring turns into early summer. One- to two-year-old lampreys move into freshwater streams. Males and females hunt out a nesting site and build a gravel and stone nest. They move the rocks by sucking them. In fact, the scientific name for sea lamprey—*Petromyzon marinus*—means "sucker of stone from the sea."

Most lampreys **spawn** when the water temperature is above 52 degrees Fahrenheit (11 degrees Celsius). The female lays from 30,000 to 200,000 eggs in the nest. The sticky eggs do not float. Then the male passes over the eggs to **fertilize** them. After producing young, both males and females become blind and die.

Eggs hatch after about two weeks, depending on the water temperature. The warmer the water, the quicker the eggs hatch. The newly hatched larvae are toothless and blind. They quickly wiggle their way downstream in search of a soft streambed. Once they find a new home in the muck, the larvae filter the water to feed on **plankton**. They live there for about three or four years.

When the lampreys change from larvae to adults, they go through a **metamorphosis**. They begin to look like

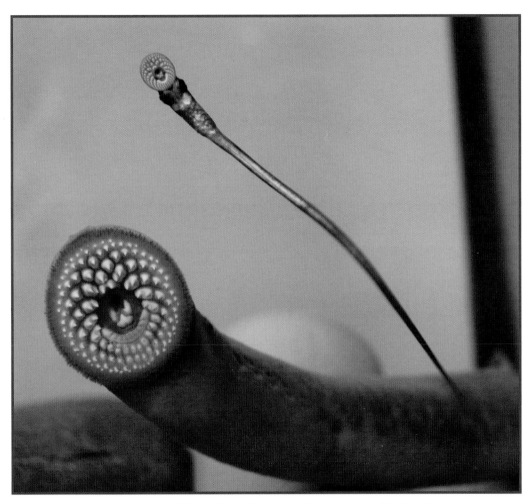

A sea lamprey adult and transformer swim next to each other in an aquarium. A sea lamprey becomes a transformer after being a larva.

adult lampreys, only much smaller. They develop teeth, eyes, and kidneys. During this stage, these young lampreys are called transformers.

The change from larva to transformer takes about four to six months. The transformer then moves out of the stream and into a larger body of water.

Adult sea lampreys normally move from freshwater streams into the Atlantic Ocean. However, lampreys that live in the Great Lakes are almost entirely surrounded by land. They never travel to the ocean, which is why they are considered animal invaders.

CHAPTER THREE

FISHY INVADER

The natural range of lampreys is in the Atlantic Ocean. It stretches from Norway south to the Mediterranean in Europe and from Labrador to Florida in North America. Lampreys that live in the ocean as adults are not harmful to their environment. Like salmon and alewives, lampreys spawn, hatch, and grow up in freshwater, but they live as adults in salt water.

Alien sea lampreys live in the Great Lakes, New York's Finger Lakes, and Lake Champlain on the Vermont-New York border. They never travel to salt water as adults, living their entire lives in freshwater. These lampreys are smaller than those that live in salt water.

There is some evidence that lampreys in the Finger Lakes and Lakes Champlain and Ontario may be native to these areas. But most scientists believe the lampreys are alien invaders because no one recorded them in Lake

Sea lampreys look like eels but aren't related to them at all. A sea lamprey in its natural range is larger than an invasive sea lamprey.

Ontario before 1830. These scientists suggest that lampreys spread through the region along the Erie Canal, which was completed in 1825.

How did sea lampreys become invaders? Sea lampreys are naturally driven to move into freshwater when it is time to spawn. Whether lampreys were native to Lake Ontario or arrived by traveling the Saint Lawrence River or the Erie Canal, they were established in the lake by 1830. But they were few and caused no problems.

Nature provided a barrier that stopped sea lampreys from moving beyond Lake Ontario. It was called Niagara Falls. Humans helped the sea lampreys overcome that barrier in time. To improve trade and transportation, humans built a canal that gave the lampreys what nature did not—a waterway into the Great Lakes.

The first Welland Canal was completed in 1829. It connected Lake Ontario to Lake Erie through the Welland River, the Niagara River, and 40 locks. (A lock is a section of a canal that is closed off with gates. Operators pump water in or out of a lock to raise or lower ships.) At that time, lampreys did not move into Lake Erie. Getting through 40 locks and lock traffic may have been too difficult.

Although sea lampreys are harmful as invaders, they are valuable in their natural habitat. As larvae, lampreys keep the water clean by feeding on plankton. The larvae also serve as food for many creatures. Lampreys that have an ocean outlet do not feed on river fish. When adult lampreys return from the ocean, they spawn and die. Their bodies provide food for other fish, dragonfly nymphs, and mammals. Sea lampreys are important in maintaining a healthy stream ecosystem. Can you think of other examples of animals depending on each other for survival in an ecosystem?

The Welland Canal received several upgrades over the years, but the lampreys stayed put. Then major improvements in the canal allowed the first sea lampreys into Lake Erie, where they were found in 1921. Again, there were few lampreys, and they did not cause serious problems.

However, another upgrade for the Welland Canal in 1932 opened the floodgates for sea lampreys. The new locks were wider and deeper. They allowed an easier passage for both ships and lampreys.

By the late 1930s, sea lampreys were living in Lakes Michigan, Huron, and Superior. The lampreys were not picky

A cargo ship exits a lock at Welland Canal in Ontario. These new locks allowed more sea lampreys to travel from Lake Ontario to Lake Erie.

eaters. They attacked every fish species in the lakes. As their populations grew, sea lampreys became a disaster for all of the Great Lakes.

CHAPTER FOUR

MANY PROBLEMS

*Here two sea lampreys have attacked a single fish. When sea
lampreys live where they don't belong, native fish species suffer.*

Sea lampreys created many problems in the Great Lakes.
Those problems developed and grew expensive quickly. An
adult sea lamprey destroys roughly 40 pounds (18 kilograms)

or more of fish during its one- to two-year life span as a parasite. The lampreys suck blood and other body fluids from their prey. The fish die from loss of blood or from infections in their wounds. Attacks are so severe that nearly 85 percent of all lamprey victims die.

Another problem is that lampreys breed in massive numbers. One estimate found more than 20,000 lampreys in just one river feeding into Lake Superior. Unfortunately, lampreys spawn in more than 400 streams.

Pollution, overfishing, and sea lampreys helped bring down the fishing industry in the three upper Great Lakes starting in the 1950s. Sea lampreys also contributed to the wiping out of native species.

The Great Lakes region depended on fishing as a major source of income. Fishery catches used to include several types of ciscoes, lake trout, walleye, yellow perch, rainbow trout, northern pike, and common carp.

In the 1950s and 1960s, fisheries failed in great numbers. Across Lakes Huron, Michigan, and Superior, lake trout catch fell from 15 million pounds (6.8 million kg) to barely 300,000 pounds (136,000 kg) in just 10 years. Fisheries closed, people lost their jobs, and the ecosystem was severely out of balance.

In addition, between overfishing and sea lampreys, three cisco species died out in Great Lakes waters. The shortnose cisco, deepwater cisco, and blackfin cisco disappeared from the upper Great Lakes.

The other cause of the cisco decline was another invasive fish species, called the alewife. Alewives arrived in the Great

An alewife has washed up on a beach in the Great Lakes. Invading alewives and sea lampreys helped wipe out three fish species in these waters.

Lakes along the same route as sea lampreys, and they liked the environment.

Lampreys contributed to the alewives' success. Food was plentiful because lampreys killed off the alewives'

major competitors. Lampreys also killed off many animals that hunted alewives. Alewives fed on cisco eggs and larvae and competed with adult ciscoes for food. Against the lampreys and the alewives, the Great Lakes ciscoes did not stand a chance.

CONTROLLING THE SEA LAMPREYS

In the 1950s, controlling the sea lampreys became a main concern for agencies in both the United States and Canada.

In the 1950s, efforts to rid the Great Lakes of sea lampreys got under way. The Great Lakes Fishery Commission (GLFC), the U.S. Fish and Wildlife Service, and Fisheries and Oceans Canada began a joint attack.

Scientists looked for and found a poison to kill off the lampreys. The poison affects sea lamprey larvae. It's used

People have used chemicals called pesticides to kill insects and other pests for many years. In the 1950s, it became clear that pesticides were killing more than just bugs. So scientists wanted to find a poison that killed lampreys but did not affect other fish, wildlife, or plant life. Scientists tested nearly 6,000 chemicals before they found what they needed. Use of any poisons in the environment demands a responsible, careful approach. Your family may use pesticides to kill bugs in your home. How might you use these chemicals as safely as possible?

where the larvae live in streams. It does not harm other creatures in the stream environment. The most effective and safe chemical is called 3-trifluoromethyl-4-nitrophenol, or TFM.

Today, 5,747 streams and rivers flow into the Great Lakes. Of those, 433 serve as sea lamprey nurseries, and 250 are treated with TFM. Because sea lamprey larvae spend four to eight years maturing, each stream is treated once every four years. The GLFC treats 60 to 70 streams yearly.

Scientists looked for other ways to control sea lampreys. Adult sea lampreys are poor swimmers. Engineers developed barriers to block spawning adults from

A fisheries biologist stands next to a barrier called a weir in Traverse City, Michigan. The weir keeps sea lampreys from spreading.

moving upstream. Most other fish can still pass through. The barriers also reduce the distance along many streams where TFM is used. This lowers the costs and increases effectiveness of TFM treatments.

Traps, often placed near barriers, catch lampreys as they travel upstream for spawning. Trapped female lampreys are used for research.

Males become part of another lamprey control program. They are injected with a chemical that makes them unable to produce offspring. Scientists release these males back into the streams where lampreys spawn. The males find mates and build nests. When the females lay their eggs, the males cannot fertilize them.

The ongoing effort to control lampreys in the Great Lakes has been a success. According to Dr. Robert Young, director of the Sea Lamprey Control Centre in Sault Sainte Marie, Ontario, "There are still hundreds of thousands of lamprey, and we'll never get rid of them totally. But we've reduced them about 90 percent

*Keeping young lampreys from spreading will help
bring back native species to the Great Lakes.*

from their original population, and we're constantly
improving techniques."

Why is successful control important? Fishery managers
can restore native species and stock popular sport fish
without fear of them being gobbled up by sea lampreys.
More important, however, by controlling the lampreys, the
lake environment is closer to returning to its natural balance.

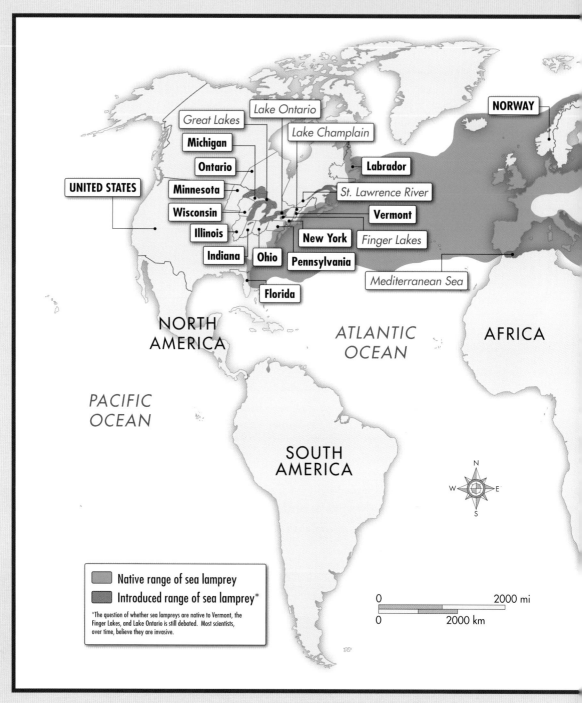

NORWAY

Lake Ontario

Great Lakes

Michigan

Lake Champlain

Ontario

Labrador

UNITED STATES

Minnesota

St. Lawrence River

Wisconsin

Vermont

Illinois

New York

Finger Lakes

Indiana

Ohio

Pennsylvania

Florida

Mediterranean Sea

NORTH
AMERICA

ATLANTIC
OCEAN

AFRICA

PACIFIC
OCEAN

SOUTH
AMERICA

N
W   E
S

Native range of sea lamprey

Introduced range of sea lamprey*

*The question of whether sea lampreys are native to Vermont, the
Finger Lakes, and Lake Ontario is still debated. Most scientists,
over time, believe they are invasive.

0   2000 mi
0   2000 km

This map shows where in the world the

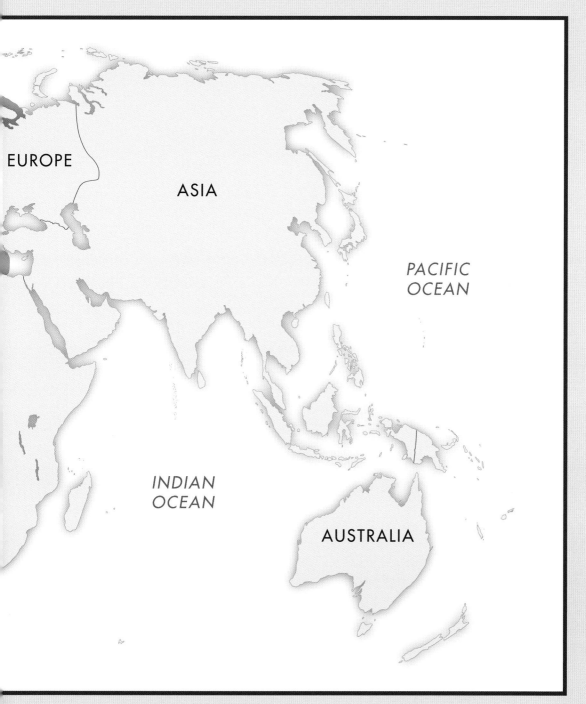

EUROPE

ASIA

PACIFIC
OCEAN

INDIAN
OCEAN

AUSTRALIA

sea lamprey lives naturally and where it has invaded.

GLOSSARY

conservationists (kon-sur-VAY-shuhn-ists) people who work to preserve, manage, and care for natural resources such as forests and wildlife

ecosystems (EE-koh-siss-tuhmz) communities of plants, animals, and other organisms together with their environment, working as a unit

fertilize (FUR-tuh-lize) to join male sperm with a female egg to create young

fisheries (FISH-ur-eez) places of business where fish or other water animals are bred or caught

habitat (HAB-ih-tat) the area where plants or animals normally live

larva (LAR-vuh) the newly hatched stage of certain animals that go through metamorphosis; more than one larva are called larvae

metamorphosis (met-uh-MOR-fuh-siss) the period of change from a larva to an adult

parasites (PEHR-uh-sites) animals or plants that live by feeding off, or living on or in, a host plant or animal

plankton (PLANGK-tuhn) tiny floating plants or animals that live in water

prey (PRAY) an animal that is eaten by another animal

spawn (SPAWN) to lay eggs and produce offspring, as some water animals do

species (SPEE-sheez) a group of similar plants or animals

transformer (trans-FORM-ur) for a sea lamprey, the stage of life after the larval stage

FOR MORE INFORMATION

Books

Fredericks, Anthony D. *Bloodsucking Creatures*. Danbury, CT: Franklin Watts, 2003.

May, Suellen. *Invasive Aquatic and Wetland Animals*. New York: Chelsea House, 2007.

Packard, Mary. *Animal Planet: The Most Extreme Predators*. San Francisco: Jossey-Bass, 2007.

Web Sites

Global Invasive Species Database: *Petromyzon marinus*
www.issg.org/database/species/ecology.asp?si=542&fr=1&sts=sss
To find out more about this invasive fish

Great Lakes Fishery Commission
www.glfc.org
To learn about what this organization does and why

Protect Your Waters
www.protectyourwaters.net/hitchhikers/fish_sea_lamprey.php
To discover why these ancient fish are a threat to some freshwater habitats

INDEX

adulthood, 8, 9, 12, 13
alewives, 20–22
aquaculture, 19, 20

carp, 19
ciscoes, 5, 19, 20, 22
color, 8
conservationists, 6, 26
control, 22, 23–27

damage, 4, 5, 18–19, 20

ecosystems, 6, 20
eggs, 10, 26
Erie Canal, 14, 15

females, 9, 10, 25, 26
fertilization, 10, 26
Finger Lakes, 13
fisheries, 6, 19–20
Fisheries and Oceans Canada, 23
freshwater, 9, 12, 13, 14–15, 22

gill pouches, 9
Great Lakes, 4–5, 5–6, 12, 13–14, 15, 16, 17, 18, 19, 20, 21, 22, 24
Great Lakes Fishery Commission (GLFC), 23, 24, 26

habitats, 6, 16, 28–29

hatching, 10, 13
Henry I, king of England, 12

infestation, 14–15, 16
invasive species, 5, 26

Lake Champlain, 13
Lake Erie, 4–5, 15, 16
Lake Huron, 16, 20
Lake Michigan, 16, 20
Lake Ontario, 13–14, 15
Lake Superior, 16, 19, 20
larvae, 9, 10, 11–12, 16, 23–24
length, 8
locks, 15

males, 9, 10, 26
mating. See spawning.
mercury, 12
metamorphosis, 10–12
Middle Ages, 12

natural range, 13
nests, 9–10, 26
Niagara Falls, 15
Niagara River, 15

parasites, 7
perch, 19
pesticides, 24
plankton, 10, 16
poisons, 23–24, 25

pollution, 6, 19
predators, 12, 16
prey, 7, 17, 19, 21–22

reproduction. See spawning.

Saint Lawrence River, 15
salmon, 22
salt water, 13
scientific name, 10
Sea Lamprey Control Centre, 26
sizes, 8
spawning, 10, 13, 15, 16, 19, 24–25, 26

teeth, 9, 11
TFM (3-trifluoromethyl-4-nitrophenol), 24, 25
tongue, 9
tourism, 6
transformers, 9, 11–12
traps, 25
trout, 5, 19, 20

U.S. Fish and Wildlife Service, 23

walleye, 4–5, 19
weight, 8
Welland Canal, 15–16
Welland River, 15

Young, Robert, 26–27

ABOUT THE AUTHOR

Barbara A. Somervill writes children's nonfiction books on a variety of topics. She is particularly interested in nature and foreign countries. Somervill believes that researching new and different topics makes writing every book an adventure. When she is not writing, Somervill is an avid reader and plays bridge.